The PRESIDENTS

PORTRAITS of HISTORY

by LEAH TINARI

ALADDIN

New York   London   Toronto   Sydney   New Delhi

To Marsden Roosie and Franco Gonzi.

I love you both so much. Thank you for giving me the independence to be myself and make art.

PS: Mars, I'm getting tired of having to give you credit and thank you for all my book ideas, so can you please cut it out? But no, seriously. Thank you, Mars, for your insatiable appetite for history. You are always my inspiration, and this book wouldn't exist without your beautiful brain.

At around the age of six, my son, Mars, became very interested in US history

and increasingly curious about the presidents. He would ask me all sorts of questions about them and want to see their images, which we would pull up on our computer and discuss. Eventually Mars wanted a visual documentation of all the presidents for his room. So we began hunting for a poster, or even single portraits of the presidents, thinking we could maybe make a border around his walls. But everything we saw felt so outdated, or sophomoric, or frankly dull. I told him there was no way I was going to buy and hang in his room anything we came across, because he would have to look at it *every day*.

I thought about it for a little while, and before truly considering the scale of the project or the time it would take, I blurted out that I would paint *all* the presidents for him myself! Well, that was silly, because once you tell Mars—or most children—something, he sure as heck holds you to it. So it began, one president at a time, one after another after another, the research, the painting, the stenciling of the text.

While creating the artwork, my hope was that these portraits would feel like a refreshing take on a thoroughly reviewed subject matter: our presidency. The portraits are meant to be serious but viewed and digested in a playful manner. The paintings are meant to bring to light the fact that before these men were elected commander in chief, they had rich and varied lives and experiences.

All were elected to a powerful position that suddenly put them into a new category—president. And the majority of citizens may forget that these people still had childhoods and mothers and fathers and favorite foods. They were fathers and sons and brothers, and had hobbies and pets.

Most important, one last point (that I hope readers will also recognize) was burned into my brain during this artistic process: the lack of diversity in race and gender of those who have governed our people for 230 years. All of these faces, except one, are monochromatic.

My hope is that this book plants a seed for not only Mars (who is now almost ten) but for everyone. Let's not ignore the many different and unique colors, shapes, and sizes in our world. I hope this review will inspire readers to want to make a change, take the blinders off, embrace diversity, and add some splashes of bold, bright color to our US story and to our future.

Before riding his horse Prescott, Washington made sure that Prescott was brushed from head to hoof and that his teeth were cleaned.

1ST

1789 to 1797

FALSE TEETH MADE OF IVORY, ANIMAL TEETH, and HUMAN TEETH

LIFELONG INTEREST IN MAP-MAKING AND GEOGRAPHY

BRED HOUND DOGS with names such as...

Tipsy
True Love
Sweet Lips

GEORGE WASHINGTON

face on MT. RUSHMORE

Adams loved the outdoors
and often skipped school
in order to hunt and fish.

Jefferson was a collector of fossils and had the bones of a mastodon sent to him.

3RD

1801 to 1809

AUTHOR OF THE DECLARATION OF INDEPENDENCE

POPULAR-IZED french fries and ice cream

THOMAS JEFFERSON

owned over 600 SLAVES

The jacket Madison wore to his inauguration was woven from the wool of sheep that were raised at Montpelier, his home in Virginia.

1809 to 1817 ·

proposed the
BILL OF
RIGHTS,
1ST 10
AMENDMENTS
to the
Constitution

4TH

and
shortest
PRESIDENT
5'4"

OLDEST of 12
BROTHERS
and SISTERS

HIS FACE
appeared
on the

$5,000
BILL

JAMES
MADISON

nickname
FATHER
of the CONSTITUTION

In 1776, Monroe dropped out of college to fight in the Revolutionary War.

1817 to 1825

5TH

his parents died when he was a TEEN-AGER

.Era of GOOD FEELINGS president

1ST DAUGHTER married in the WHITE HOUSE

SHOT and lived

JAMES MONROE

1ST PRESIDENT to sail on a STEAMBOAT

During his presidency, early in the morning Adams enjoyed skinny-dipping in the Potomac River.

6 TH

was rumored to have worn the same hat FOR **10** YEARS

alligator at the WHITE HOUSE

wife, LOUISA, raised silkworms AND used silk for her gowns

liked to SKINNY-DIP

1825 to 1829

JOHN QUINCY ADAMS

nickname OLD MAN ELOQUENT

Jackson was a practical joker when he was young and would move people's outhouses during the night so that they couldn't find them.

1829 to 1837

was BORN in a LOG CABIN

fought OVER 100 DUELS

BATTLE OF THE ALAMO

7TH

on the $20 BILL

1ST PRESIDENT to ride a STEAM-POWERED train

ANDREW JACKSON

his PET PARROT liked to CURSE

Van Buren attended a one-room schoolhouse until age fourteen.

Harrison was the only president who studied to become a doctor.

1841 to 1841

9TH

served ONLY 31 days in office

DIED of TYPHOID FEVER contracted through the contaminated WHITE HOUSE water system.

had 10 children

LONGEST inaugural speech, almost 2 hrs

WILLIAM HENRY HARRISON

"the strongest of all government IS THAT which is MOST FREE."

Tyler had fifteen children—
eight with his first wife,
Letitia, and seven with his
second wife, Julia.

10TH 1841 to 1845

nickname his ACCIDENCY

HE WAS 70 YEARS OLD WHEN his 15TH child was BORN

played the VIOLIN

JOHN TYLER

named his plantation SHERWOOD FOREST after ROBIN Hood

While president, Polk often worked twelve or more hours a day and only rarely took vacation.

11TH

1845 to 1849

banned DANCING from the White House

GRANTED statehood to TEXAS!

54° 40' or FIGHT

negotiated with British for the areas now.

OREGON, IDAHO, and WASHINGTON

JAMES K. POLK

INCREASED the size of the US BY 1/3

Taylor enjoyed chewing tobacco and was a precise shot when aiming for a spittoon.

1849 to 1850

12TH

LAST US president to own slaves in the WHITE HOUSE!

he got sick and DIED after having MILK and CHERRIES

nickname OLD ROUGH and READY

ZACHARY TAYLOR

liked to wear MISMATCHED clothing

Fillmore and his wife, Abigail, started the first White House library; it had about two hundred books.

13TH
1850 to 1853
BORN IN A LOG CABIN
TAUGHT HIMSELF TO READ
he created the 1ST LIBRARY in the WHITE HOUSE
MILLARD FILLMORE

Pierce was the first president to recite his inaugural address from memory, without any notes.

1853 to 1857

14TH

he introduced the CHRISTMAS TREE to the WHITE HOUSE!

RAN AWAY FROM SCHOOL

FRANKLIN PIERCE

Buchanan enrolled in
Dickinson College
at age sixteen.

15 TH. 1857 to 1861

NICKNAME
10¢ JIMMY

his niece
HARRIET
was the
HOSTESS
AT
WHITE
HOUSE
events !!

NEVER
MARRIED

he enjoyed
EATING
FRENCH
FOOD

JAMES
BUCHANAN

NEARSIGHTED in 1 EYE   FARSIGHTED in the other

Lincoln invented a device to lift boats grounded in shallow water, making him the only president to hold a patent (number 6469).

16TH

1861 to 1865
issued the
EMANCIPATION
PROCLAMATION
to FREE
slaves

AND

TALLEST

president
AND a
face on.

MT. RUSHMORE

Made
Turkey
day a
HOLIDAY

assassinated
by JOHN
WILKES
BOOTH

ABRAHAM LINCOLN

Johnson was trained
as a tailor and owned
a tailor shop before he
was president.

A favorite breakfast of Grant's was a cucumber soaked in vinegar.

18 TH · 1869 to 1877

he wore FALSE TEETH

ARRESTED for speeding while DRIVING his HORSE AND BUGGY

$

ON THE $50 BILL $$

ULYSSES S. GRANT

The White House Easter
Egg Roll was started by
Hayes and his wife, Lucy.

19TH **1877 to 1881**

HAD THE **1ST**

telephone installed in the WHITE HOUSE

THE PHONE NUMBER WAS

#1

ring ring ring

1st person he called was ALEXANDER graham BELL

RUTHERFORD B. HAYES

Garfield could simultaneously write in Greek with one hand and in Latin with the other.

20TH

1881 to 1881

200 days in OFFICE

worked as a JANITOR to PAY for HIS COLLEGE classes

HAD A DOG named VETO

LEFT-HANDED

JAMES GARFIELD

HE DREAMED of being a SAILOR

While attending Union College, as a prank Arthur helped throw the school bell into the Erie Canal.

21ST

1881 to 1885

nickname
ELEGANT
ARTHUR
the
MOST
WELL-
dressed
PRESIDENT

PLAYED

THE

BANJO

CHESTER A. ARTHUR

(OWNED) more than 80 PAIRS of PANTS

Cleveland was the only president to serve nonconsecutive terms.

McKinley loved red carnations and often wore one on his lapel to bring him good luck.

23RD 1889 to 1893
the "centennial president" he was

1st president to attend A PROFESSIONAL BASEBALL GAME

INAUGURATED 100 YEARS AFTER GW

BENJAMIN HARRISON

HE LIKED BOOKS MORE than people!

When Harrison's pet goat, Old Whiskers, got away with his grandson in a cart, Harrison chased them through Washington, DC.

25TH 1897 to 1901

1ST president TO RIDE in an AUTOMOBILE

he had A PET PARROT that WHISTLED YANKEE DOODLE

vroom vroom

WILLIAM McKINLEY

the LAST president to have served in the CIVIL WAR

Roosevelt could walk on stilts, and others in his family had their own pairs.

26TH 1901 to 1909 allocated 230 million ACRES to be Preserved AS Public land

1ST AMERICAN TO WIN the NOBEL PEACE PRIZE

he went UP in an AIRPLANE and DOWN in a SUBMARINE

face on MT. RUSHMORE

THEODORE (AKA TEDDY) ROOSEVELT

Taft enjoyed fresh milk in the morning and kept a cow on the White House lawn.

27TH 1909 to 1913

1ST
PRESIDENT to throw

nicknamed

BIG BILL
due to HIS
LARGE SIZE

1ST PITCH at a Professional BASEBALL GAME

WILLIAM HOWARD TAFT

kept a COW on the WHITE HOUSE LAWN

Wilson didn't learn the alphabet until he was nine and couldn't read until a few years later.

1913 to 1921
WWI
BROKE
OUT
IN
EUROPE

28 TH

HE WAS DYSLEXIC

LOVED
to golf
in the
WINTER,
painted golf
balls BLACK so
he could find
them in the SNOW

ON THE
$100.K
BILL

WOODROW
WILSON

Harding played the tuba and would often rehearse with the United States Marine Band.

29TH 1921 to 1923

1ST president to have HIS VOICE BROADCAST LIVE VIA RADIO

HE WORE SIZE 14 SHOES !!!

WARREN G. HARDING

While eating breakfast in bed, Coolidge liked having his scalp massaged with petroleum jelly.

1923 to 1929
nickname SILENT CAL
SLOGAN ...
keep
COOL
WITH
COOLIDGE

30
TH
period
OF
prosperity
ROARING
20s

HE
PLAYED
THE
HARMONICA
AND
LOVED
pancakes !!

HAD 2
PET
RACCOONS

CALVIN
COOLIDGE

To keep Hoover in shape, his
doctor invented Hooverball,
a game that's a combination
of tennis and volleyball and
uses a medicine ball.

31ST 1929 to 1933

THE STOCK MARKET CRASH triggered THE GREAT DEPRESSION

WAS an ORPHAN at age 9!

MADE "The STAR-SPANGLED BANNER" the national anthem

HERBERT HOOVER

Roosevelt loved to collect stamps and had more than one million stamps in his collection.

1933 to 1945
HE WAS ELECTED
for 4 TERMS

HE
INSTITUTED
the
NEW
DEAL

the ONLY
thing we
have to
FEAR is
FEAR
itself

32
ND

WWII
BROKE
OUT!

PEARL
HARBOR

FRANKLIN D.
ROOSEVELT

In honor of Truman's sixty-third birthday, a bowling alley was installed in the West Wing of the White House.

33RD • 1945 to 1953

nickname

GIVE
'EM
HELL
HARRY

dropped
THE ATOMIC
BOMB

HARRY S
TRUMAN

PLAYED
THE PIANO
!!!!!!!

Eisenhower changed the name of the presidential retreat in Maryland from Shangri-La to Camp David, in honor of his grandson.

34TH

1953 to 1961

(is supreme commander in WWII he planned the INVASION OF NORMANDY

D-DAY

HE LOVED to cook!

nickname IKE

CAMPAIGN SLOGAN "I LIKE IKE"

DWIGHT D. EISENHOWER

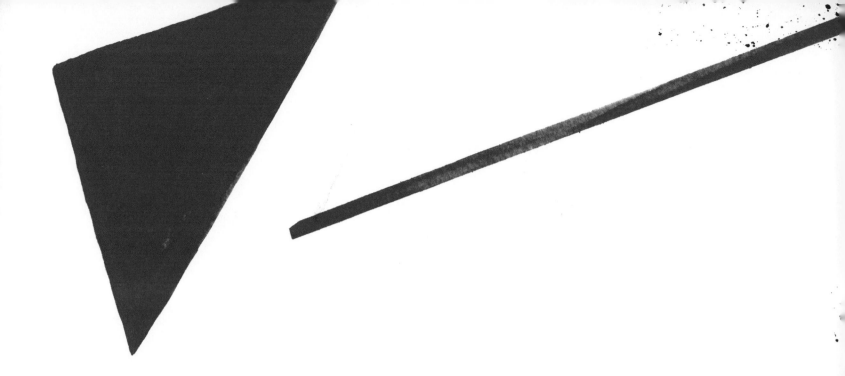

Kennedy was the last president to wear a top hat to his inauguration.

1961 to 1963
35TH
he was a BOY SCOUT!!
started the PEACE CORPS
FAMOUS WORDS: "ASK NOT what your country can do for you; ASK what YOU can do for your COUNTRY"
YOUNGEST president to be ASSASSINATED
BAY OF PIGS
JOHN F. KENNEDY
(AKA JFK, JACK)
LOVED PLAYING TOUCH FOOTBALL

Johnson married Claudia Alta Taylor (also known as Lady Bird) with a $2.50 wedding ring from Sears.

Nixon played saxophone, clarinet, accordion, violin, and piano but couldn't read sheet music.

Ford was an Eagle Scout
in the Boy Scouts and
loved football, boxing,
skiing, and golf.

38TH 1974 to 1977

HE narrowly ESCAPED DEATH during a typhoon IN the SOUTH PACIFIC during WWII

WAS A GREAT FOOTBALL PLAYER AND A FASHION MODEL

LOVED TO SMOKE HIS PIPE AND E... butter pecan ice cream

GERALD FORD

Carter was the only
president to officially
report seeing a UFO.

Reagan was a cheerleader at Eureka College in Eureka, Illinois.

40 TH 1981 to 1989

WAS A HOLLYWOOD MOVIE STAR!

LOVED JELLY BEANS

RONALD REAGAN

was shot by an assassin and lived

REAGANOMICS

Bush celebrated his seventy-fifth, eightieth, eighty-fifth, *and* ninetieth birthdays by going skydiving.

1989 to 1993
was the
irector
of the
CIA
NAVY fighter PILOT
INVADED PANAMA AND CAPTURED NORIEGA
41 ST
HATED
BROCCOLI
GEORGE H.W. BUSH

Clinton designed a *New York Times* crossword with the theme Twistin' the Oldies.

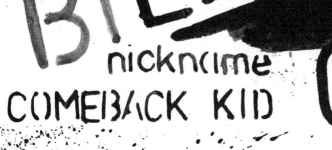

42

1993 to 2001

42ND

loves KRISPY KREME

HE ENJOYS PLAYING THE SAXOPHONE

1 OF THE longest periods of PEACE AND ECONOMIC EXPANSION in AMERICAN HISTORY !!

BILL

CLINTON

nickname COMEBACK KID

After his presidency Bush began to paint portraits, but he kept his hobby a secret from the public in the beginning.

Obama grew up loving comic books and collected Spider-Man and Conan the Barbarian comics.

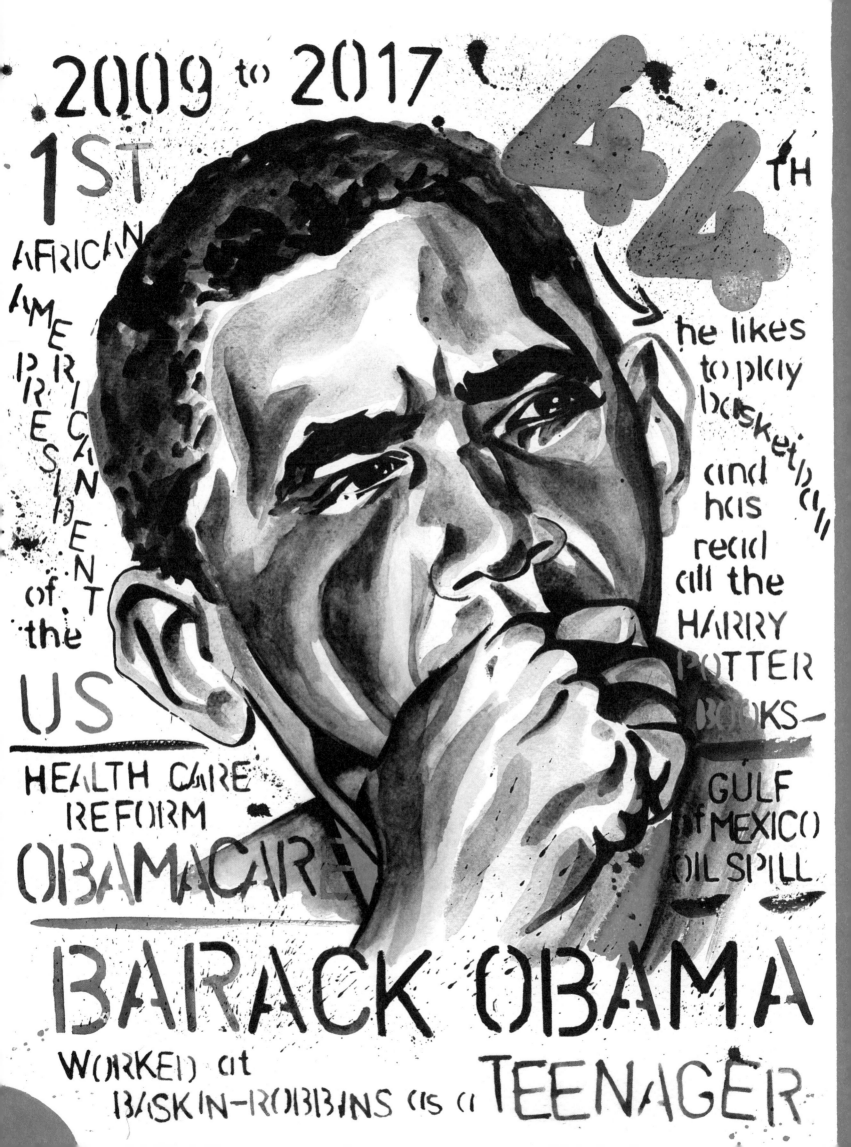

Trump has a star on the Hollywood Walk of Fame.

45TH
2017
SLOGAN MAKE AMERICA GREAT AGAIN!
LOVES GOLFING
REALITY TV SHOW
FAKE NEWS
HAS 5 CHILDREN
LOVES DIET COKE, CORNFLAKES, and McDonald's.
TWEETER
DONALD TRUMP
HOSTED WRESTLEMANIA in 1988 and 1989

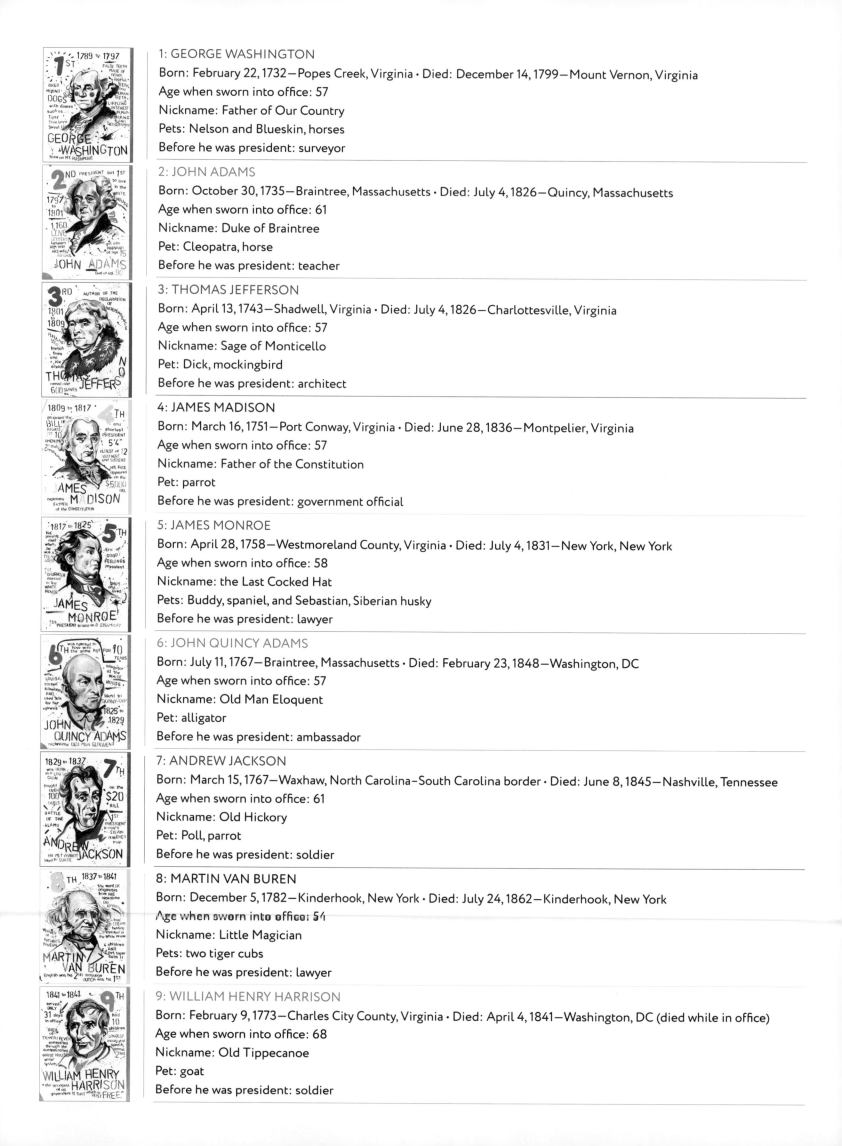

1: GEORGE WASHINGTON

Born: February 22, 1732—Popes Creek, Virginia · Died: December 14, 1799—Mount Vernon, Virginia

Age when sworn into office: 57

Nickname: Father of Our Country

Pets: Nelson and Blueskin, horses

Before he was president: surveyor

2: JOHN ADAMS

Born: October 30, 1735—Braintree, Massachusetts · Died: July 4, 1826—Quincy, Massachusetts

Age when sworn into office: 61

Nickname: Duke of Braintree

Pet: Cleopatra, horse

Before he was president: teacher

3: THOMAS JEFFERSON

Born: April 13, 1743—Shadwell, Virginia · Died: July 4, 1826—Charlottesville, Virginia

Age when sworn into office: 57

Nickname: Sage of Monticello

Pet: Dick, mockingbird

Before he was president: architect

4: JAMES MADISON

Born: March 16, 1751—Port Conway, Virginia · Died: June 28, 1836—Montpelier, Virginia

Age when sworn into office: 57

Nickname: Father of the Constitution

Pet: parrot

Before he was president: government official

5: JAMES MONROE

Born: April 28, 1758—Westmoreland County, Virginia · Died: July 4, 1831—New York, New York

Age when sworn into office: 58

Nickname: the Last Cocked Hat

Pets: Buddy, spaniel, and Sebastian, Siberian husky

Before he was president: lawyer

6: JOHN QUINCY ADAMS

Born: July 11, 1767—Braintree, Massachusetts · Died: February 23, 1848—Washington, DC

Age when sworn into office: 57

Nickname: Old Man Eloquent

Pet: alligator

Before he was president: ambassador

7: ANDREW JACKSON

Born: March 15, 1767—Waxhaw, North Carolina–South Carolina border · Died: June 8, 1845—Nashville, Tennessee

Age when sworn into office: 61

Nickname: Old Hickory

Pet: Poll, parrot

Before he was president: soldier

8: MARTIN VAN BUREN

Born: December 5, 1782—Kinderhook, New York · Died: July 24, 1862—Kinderhook, New York

Age when sworn into office: 54

Nickname: Little Magician

Pets: two tiger cubs

Before he was president: lawyer

9: WILLIAM HENRY HARRISON

Born: February 9, 1773—Charles City County, Virginia · Died: April 4, 1841—Washington, DC (died while in office)

Age when sworn into office: 68

Nickname: Old Tippecanoe

Pet: goat

Before he was president: soldier

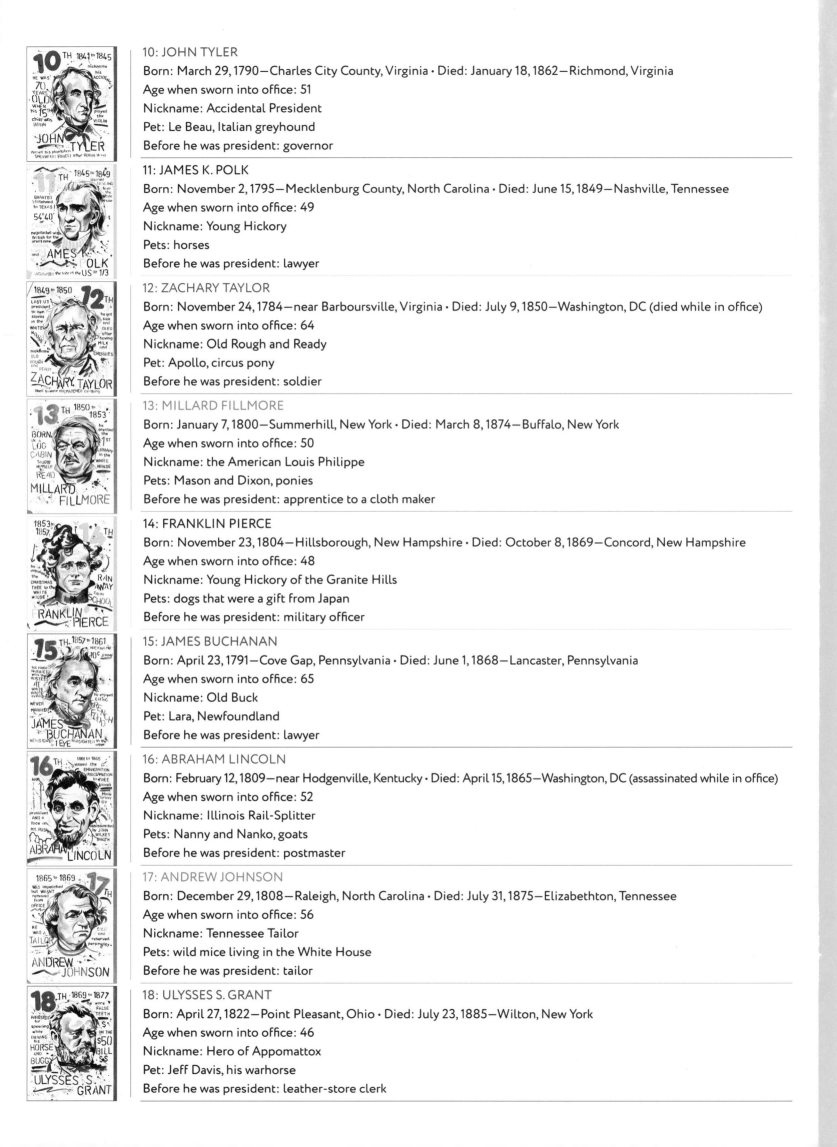

10: JOHN TYLER

Born: March 29, 1790—Charles City County, Virginia · Died: January 18, 1862—Richmond, Virginia

Age when sworn into office: 51

Nickname: Accidental President

Pet: Le Beau, Italian greyhound

Before he was president: governor

11: JAMES K. POLK

Born: November 2, 1795—Mecklenburg County, North Carolina · Died: June 15, 1849—Nashville, Tennessee

Age when sworn into office: 49

Nickname: Young Hickory

Pets: horses

Before he was president: lawyer

12: ZACHARY TAYLOR

Born: November 24, 1784—near Barboursville, Virginia · Died: July 9, 1850—Washington, DC (died while in office)

Age when sworn into office: 64

Nickname: Old Rough and Ready

Pet: Apollo, circus pony

Before he was president: soldier

13: MILLARD FILLMORE

Born: January 7, 1800—Summerhill, New York · Died: March 8, 1874—Buffalo, New York

Age when sworn into office: 50

Nickname: the American Louis Philippe

Pets: Mason and Dixon, ponies

Before he was president: apprentice to a cloth maker

14: FRANKLIN PIERCE

Born: November 23, 1804—Hillsborough, New Hampshire · Died: October 8, 1869—Concord, New Hampshire

Age when sworn into office: 48

Nickname: Young Hickory of the Granite Hills

Pets: dogs that were a gift from Japan

Before he was president: military officer

15: JAMES BUCHANAN

Born: April 23, 1791—Cove Gap, Pennsylvania · Died: June 1, 1868—Lancaster, Pennsylvania

Age when sworn into office: 65

Nickname: Old Buck

Pet: Lara, Newfoundland

Before he was president: lawyer

16: ABRAHAM LINCOLN

Born: February 12, 1809—near Hodgenville, Kentucky · Died: April 15, 1865—Washington, DC (assassinated while in office)

Age when sworn into office: 52

Nickname: Illinois Rail-Splitter

Pets: Nanny and Nanko, goats

Before he was president: postmaster

17: ANDREW JOHNSON

Born: December 29, 1808—Raleigh, North Carolina · Died: July 31, 1875—Elizabethton, Tennessee

Age when sworn into office: 56

Nickname: Tennessee Tailor

Pets: wild mice living in the White House

Before he was president: tailor

18: ULYSSES S. GRANT

Born: April 27, 1822—Point Pleasant, Ohio · Died: July 23, 1885—Wilton, New York

Age when sworn into office: 46

Nickname: Hero of Appomattox

Pet: Jeff Davis, his warhorse

Before he was president: leather-store clerk

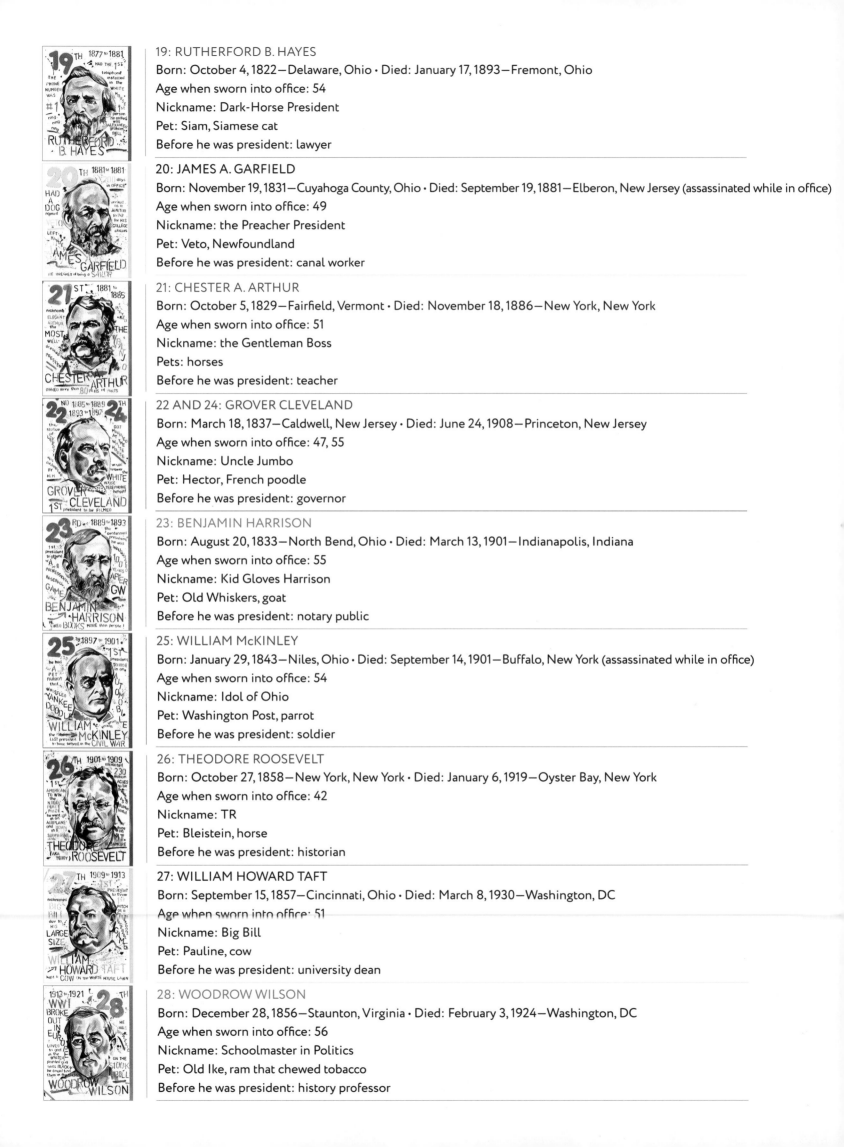

19: RUTHERFORD B. HAYES

Born: October 4, 1822—Delaware, Ohio · Died: January 17, 1893—Fremont, Ohio

Age when sworn into office: 54

Nickname: Dark-Horse President

Pet: Siam, Siamese cat

Before he was president: lawyer

20: JAMES A. GARFIELD

Born: November 19, 1831—Cuyahoga County, Ohio · Died: September 19, 1881—Elberon, New Jersey (assassinated while in office)

Age when sworn into office: 49

Nickname: the Preacher President

Pet: Veto, Newfoundland

Before he was president: canal worker

21: CHESTER A. ARTHUR

Born: October 5, 1829—Fairfield, Vermont · Died: November 18, 1886—New York, New York

Age when sworn into office: 51

Nickname: the Gentleman Boss

Pets: horses

Before he was president: teacher

22 AND 24: GROVER CLEVELAND

Born: March 18, 1837—Caldwell, New Jersey · Died: June 24, 1908—Princeton, New Jersey

Age when sworn into office: 47, 55

Nickname: Uncle Jumbo

Pet: Hector, French poodle

Before he was president: governor

23: BENJAMIN HARRISON

Born: August 20, 1833—North Bend, Ohio · Died: March 13, 1901—Indianapolis, Indiana

Age when sworn into office: 55

Nickname: Kid Gloves Harrison

Pet: Old Whiskers, goat

Before he was president: notary public

25: WILLIAM McKINLEY

Born: January 29, 1843—Niles, Ohio · Died: September 14, 1901—Buffalo, New York (assassinated while in office)

Age when sworn into office: 54

Nickname: Idol of Ohio

Pet: Washington Post, parrot

Before he was president: soldier

26: THEODORE ROOSEVELT

Born: October 27, 1858—New York, New York · Died: January 6, 1919—Oyster Bay, New York

Age when sworn into office: 42

Nickname: TR

Pet: Bleistein, horse

Before he was president: historian

27: WILLIAM HOWARD TAFT

Born: September 15, 1857—Cincinnati, Ohio · Died: March 8, 1930—Washington, DC

Age when sworn into office: 51

Nickname: Big Bill

Pet: Pauline, cow

Before he was president: university dean

28: WOODROW WILSON

Born: December 28, 1856—Staunton, Virginia · Died: February 3, 1924—Washington, DC

Age when sworn into office: 56

Nickname: Schoolmaster in Politics

Pet: Old Ike, ram that chewed tobacco

Before he was president: history professor

29: WARREN G. HARDING

Born: November 2, 1865—Corsica, Ohio · Died: August 2, 1923—San Francisco, California (died while in office)

Age when sworn into office: 55

Nickname: Wobbly Warren

Pet: Pete, squirrel

Before he was president: newspaper editor

30: CALVIN COOLIDGE

Born: July 4, 1872—Plymouth Notch, Vermont · Died: January 5, 1933—Northampton, Massachusetts

Age when sworn into office: 51

Nickname: Silent Cal

Pets: raccoons

Before he was president: governor

31: HERBERT HOOVER

Born: August 10, 1874—West Branch, Iowa · Died: October 20, 1964—New York, New York

Age when sworn into office: 54

Nickname: the Great Engineer

Pet: King Tut, Belgian shepherd

Before he was president: mining engineer

32: FRANKLIN D. ROOSEVELT

Born: January 30, 1882—Hyde Park, New York · Died: April 12, 1945—Warm Springs, Georgia (died while in office)

Age when sworn into office: 51

Nickname: FDR

Pet: Meggie, Scottish terrier

Before he was president: lawyer

33: HARRY S. TRUMAN

Born: May 8, 1884—Lamar, Missouri · Died: December 26, 1972—Kansas City, Missouri

Age when sworn into office: 60

Nickname: Give 'Em Hell Harry

Pet: Feller, cocker spaniel

Before he was president: railroad timekeeper

34: DWIGHT D. EISENHOWER

Born: October 14, 1890—Denison, Texas · Died: March 28, 1969—Washington, DC

Age when sworn into office: 62

Nickname: Ike

Pets: Gabby, parakeet, and Heidi, Weimaraner

Before he was president: university president

35: JOHN F. KENNEDY

Born: May 29, 1917—Brookline, Massachusetts · Died: November 22, 1963—Dallas, Texas (assassinated while in office)

Age when sworn into office: 43

Nickname: Jack

Pet: Zsa Zsa, rabbit

Before he was president: military officer

36: LYNDON B. JOHNSON

Born: August 27, 1908—Stonewall, Texas · Died: January 22, 1973—Stonewall, Texas

Age when sworn into office: 55

Nickname: LBJ

Pets: Him and Her, beagles

Before he was president: rancher

37: RICHARD NIXON

Born: January 9, 1913—Yorba Linda, California · Died: April 22, 1994—New York, New York

Age when sworn into office: 56

Nickname: Tricky Dick

Pet: Vicky, French poodle

Before he was president: lawyer

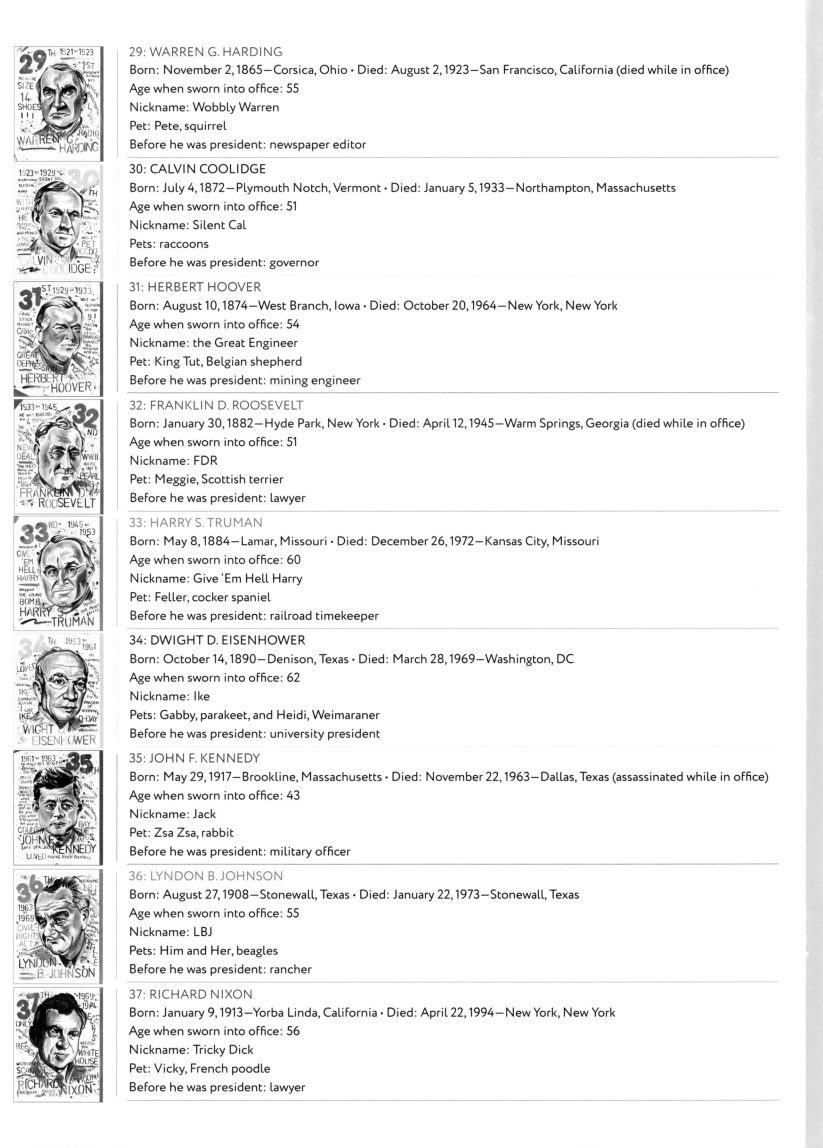

38: GERALD FORD

Born: July 14, 1913—Omaha, Nebraska · Died: December 26, 2006—Rancho Mirage, California

Age when sworn into office: 61

Nickname: Jerry

Pet: Liberty, golden retriever

Before he was president: lawyer

39: JIMMY CARTER

Born: October 1, 1924—Plains, Georgia

Age when sworn into office: 52

Nickname: the Peanut Farmer

Pet: Misty Malarky Ying Yang, Siamese cat

Before he was president: farmer

40: RONALD REAGAN

Born: February 6, 1911—Tampico, Illinois · Died: June 5, 2004—Los Angeles, California

Age when sworn into office: 69

Nickname: the Gipper

Pet: Rex, King Charles spaniel

Before he was president: radio announcer

41: GEORGE H. W. BUSH

Born: June 12, 1924—Milton, Massachusetts · Died: November 30, 2018—Houston, Texas

Age when sworn into office: 64

Nickname: Poppy

Pet: Millie, English springer spaniel

Before he was president: military officer

42: BILL CLINTON

Born: August 19, 1946—Hope, Arkansas

Age when sworn into office: 46

Nickname: Bubba

Pets: Socks, cat, and Buddy, chocolate Lab

Before he was president: governor

43: GEORGE W. BUSH

Born: July 6, 1946—New Haven, Connecticut

Age when sworn into office: 54

Nickname: Dubya

Pets: Barney and Miss Beazley, Scottish terriers

Before he was president: part owner of Texas Rangers

44: BARACK OBAMA

Born: August 4, 1961—Honolulu, Hawaii

Age when sworn into office: 47

Nickname: No-Drama Obama

Pets: Bo and Sunny, Portuguese water dogs

Before he was president: community organizer

45: DONALD TRUMP

Born: June 14, 1946—New York, New York

Age when sworn into office: 70

Nickname: the Donald

Pets: none

Before he was president: businessman